WHAT IS A CONSTELLATION?

LAURA LORIA

Britannica
Educational Publishing

IN ASSOCIATION WITH

ROSEN
EDUCATIONAL SERVICES

Published in 2015 by Britannica Educational Publishing (a trademark of Encyclopædia Britannica, Inc.) in association with The Rosen Publishing Group, Inc.
29 East 21st Street, New York, NY 10010

Distributed exclusively by Rosen Publishing.
To see additional Britannica Educational Publishing titles, go to rosenpublishing.com.

First Edition

Britannica Educational Publishing
J. E. Luebering: Director, Core Reference Group
Mary Rose McCudden: Editor, Britannica Student Encyclopedia

Rosen Publishing
Hope Lourie Killcoyne: Executive Editor
Jeanne Nagle: Editor
Nelson Sá: Art Director
Michael Moy: Designer
Cindy Reiman: Photography Manager
Marty Levick: Photo Researcher

Cataloging-in-Publication Data

Loria, Laura.
What is a constellation?/Laura Loria.
      pages cm. — (Let's find out! Space)
Audience: Grades 3-6.
Includes bibliographical references and index.
ISBN 978-1-62275-476-2 (library bound) — ISBN 978-1-62275-478-6 (pbk.) — ISBN 978-1-62275-479-3 (6-pack)
1. Constellations — Juvenile literature. 2. Solar system — Juvenile literature. 3. Mythology, Classical — Juvenile literature. I. Title.
QB801.7.N34 2015
523.8 — dc23

2014001955

Manufactured in the United States of America

Photo Credits
Cover (constellation) © iStockphoto.com/sololos; cover, p. 1, interior pages background (clouds and stars) MarcelClemens/Shutterstock.com; p. 4 tharrison/iStock Vectors/Getty Images; p. 5 John G. Zimmerman/Sports Illustrated/Getty Images; p. 6 Universal History Archive/Universal Images Group/Getty Images; p. 7 Werner Forman/Universal Images Group/Getty Images; p. 8 Library of Congress, Washington, D.C. (Digital file no. LC-DIG-ds-00241); p. 9 Library of Congress, Washington, D.C. (file no. LC-USZC4-10062); pp. 10, 18 Science & Society Picture Library/Getty Images; pp. 11, 19 Buyenlarge/Archive Photos/Getty Images; p. 12 Tomacco/iStock Vectors/Getty Images; p. 13 Image Work/ amanaimagesRF/Thinkstock; p. 14 Mondadori Portfolio/Hulton Fine Art Collection/Getty Images; p. 15 John Davis/Stocktrek Images/Getty Images; p. 16 Encyclopædia Britannica, Inc.; p. 17 Barcroft Media/Getty Images; p. 20 Jan Tyler/E+/Getty Images; p. 21 Science Museum/SSPL/ Getty Images; pp. 22, 26 The Bridgeman Art Library/Getty Images; p. 23 Library of Congress, Washington, D.C. (file no. LC-USZC4-10060); p. 24 Library of Congress, Washington, D.C. (file no. LC-USZC4-10063); p. 25 Malte Mueller/Getty Images; p. 27 Jay M. Pasachoff/Science Faction/ Getty Images; p. 28 Erkki Makkonen/E+/Getty Images; p. 29 Babak Tafreshi/Photo Researchers/ Getty Images.

CONTENTS

Pictures in the Sky

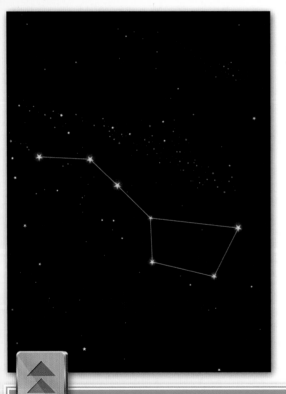

For thousands of years, people have looked at stars and identified patterns. Connecting the stars in their minds, people saw imaginary pictures of animals and objects. These star patterns are called **constellations**.

In scientific terms, constellations are not real. The stars in constellations

The Big Dipper is an easily seen pattern in the night sky.

are often very far away from each other and therefore not close enough to form patterns. They only appear close together to us on Earth.

Constellations are like a map, making it an easy way for scientists to locate certain stars in the sky. They have also been used for navigation on land and at sea for ages. Many cultures have built legends and stories around constellations, giving them special meaning.

The word "**constellation**" comes from two Latin words: *con*, meaning "with," and *stella*, meaning "star."

A sailor can navigate by looking at the stars.

ANCIENT MESOPOTAMIA

In 3300 BCE, a group of nomads, or wanderers, called the Sumerians settled in Mesopotamia, which is in modern-day Iraq. It was there that the first civilizations were formed. Historians think they also were the first people who named star patterns in the sky. Historians believe that the Sumerians named the constellations after the animals

This painting depicts rams being led into the Sumerian city of Ur.

THINK ABOUT IT

Imagine you lived in ancient Mesopotamia. Would you keep a record of what you saw in the sky?

An ancient Sumerian record, with drawings and cuneiform *(right)*.

living around them, such as bulls, rams, and lions.

The Sumerians kept written records by drawing pictures on clay tablets, writing in a system called cuneiform. They recorded their observations about the Sun, Moon, and other stars. Their records and legends were passed on to other people who settled in the same area, including the Babylonians and Assyrians.

ANCIENT GREECE

Beginning around the fourth century BCE, ancient Greek astronomers kept detailed records of their observations of stars. They built on the knowledge of the Mesopotamians to make their own list of constellations. Some kept the same original animal names, only translated into Greek or Latin. For example, the Babylonian constellation Mul Ur Gu La was renamed

This drawing shows how the Leo constellations look like lions.

Leo in Greek. Both names mean "lion."

The Greeks tied legends and myths from their culture to constellations. According to legend, the god Zeus placed the constellation Delphinus, the dolphin, in the sky as a way to honor the dolphin that saved a famous Greek poet from drowning.

The dolphin constellation Delphinus *(upper left)*.

DELPHINUS, SAGITTA, AQUILA. Pl. 13.

AND ANTINOUS.

Ptolemy's List

In the year 150 CE, an astronomer from Egypt named Ptolemy (toll-em-ee) created a written work about the contents of the sky. Divided into 13 books, the work included a plan of the solar system, mathematical ideas, and information on celestial objects such as the Moon, Sun, and stars.

Ptolemy *(left)*, shown using special tools and guided by the goddess Astronomia.

Aquarius The Water Bearer

Aquarius is one of the constellations on Ptolemy's original list.

Ptolemy listed 48 constellations, all of which are still recognized today. His list was not perfect or complete. It included only the constellations he could see from his part of the world. The work was translated into Arabic and Latin, and it was the main guide for astronomers for many centuries.

THINK ABOUT IT

Why was it important for Ptolemy to create his list? How did it help future astronomers?

THE ZODIAC

Twelve constellations on Ptolemy's list had extra-special meaning. These have become the zodiac, or circle of animals. The constellations of the zodiac are positioned in a ring around Earth. Ancient Greeks and Romans tracked the movement of these constellations through the sky based on where they were in relation to the Sun. They recorded the dates that

The twelve signs of the zodiac, shown on a wheel chart.

THINK ABOUT IT

Some people believe that the constellations of the zodiac affect how people act and what their futures will be.

these constellations were due to appear.

There are detailed legends about each constellation in the zodiac. For example, Capricorn is supposedly a goat that jumped into a river to escape the monster Typhon.

Capricorn is sometimes called a "sea-goat" because of the constellation's fish tail.

Star Maps

Constellations have a variety of practical uses. Before there were calendars, farmers could tell when the seasons would change by how and where constellations appeared in the sky.

Constellations are also useful for

An illustration shows the zodiac figures blowing seasonal winds toward farmers working the land *(center)*.

navigation. A group of stars called the Big Dipper, in the constellation Ursa Major, points to the star called Polaris, or the North Star. Early navigators learned to use the position of Polaris to find their way as they traveled.

COMPARE AND CONTRAST

How do stars compare to an electronic navigation device, such as GPS? What are the strengths and weaknesses of each method?

Interestingly the North Star is not one of the brightest stars in the night sky.

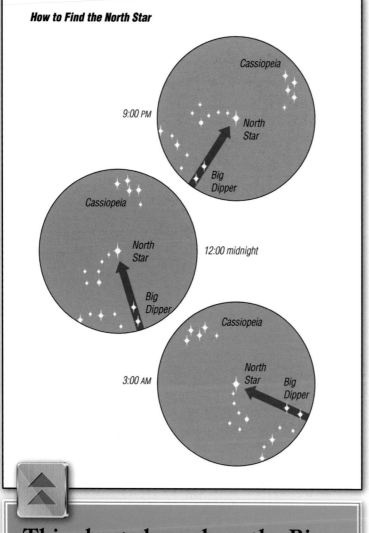

How to Find the North Star

Cassiopeia

9:00 PM

North Star

Big Dipper

Cassiopeia

North Star

12:00 midnight

Big Dipper

3:00 AM

Cassiopeia

North Star

Big Dipper

This chart shows how the Big Dipper stars always point to the North Star.

To astronomers, constellations are not just pictures in the sky. They are used to locate where other objects in space can be found. Although each constellation has stars that make up its shape, any star located within that pattern is part of the constellation. Saying that a star is in a constellation is a simple way to explain that star's location.

Capella, shown over Mount Everest, is ranked as the sixth-brightest star.

Stars are sometimes named according to the constellation in which they are found. The brightest stars in a constellation are named with Greek letters comparing them to other stars in the constellation.

THE MODERN LIST OF CONSTELLATIONS

Ptolemy's list of constellations was limited by what he himself could observe. Over time, more constellations were named as they were observed from different parts of the world. Scientists did not always agree on which star groups were official constellations. But in the 20th century, astronomers around the world shared information to create

This 18th-century globe shows the position of constellations visible around the world.

a complete list of constellations, which included those described by Ptolemy.

A group called the International Astronomical Union, or the IAU, created this official list in 1922. They chose the constellations that were most commonly known at the time. Today's list includes 88 constellations named after characters and creatures from myths, as well as animals and objects.

THINK ABOUT IT
What problems might occur if scientists cannot agree on a list of constellations?

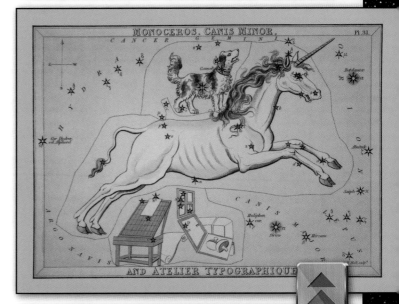

The Canis Minor ("Lesser Dog") and Monoceros ("Unicorn") constellations are depicted in this print.

Northern and Southern Constellations

Earth is divided into two **hemispheres**, or halves. Ptolemy lived in the Northern Hemisphere, so his list included only the constellations that he could see from there. He did not realize that there were constellations that he could not see.

Most constellations can be seen by people in both hemispheres, but some

This star map shows constellations of the Northern Hemisphere.

The word **hemisphere** comes from the Greek words *hemi* ("half") and *sphaira* ("sphere").

can be seen only from the Northern Hemisphere and some only from the Southern Hemisphere. The zodiac constellations are in the ecliptic, which is the path the Sun takes as it crosses the sky throughout the year.

Depending on where one lives, different constellations appear at different times of the year. This is because Earth orbits around the Sun, and the view of the sky changes as Earth moves.

This star map shows constellations of the Southern Hemisphere.

CONSTELLATIONS IN SPRING

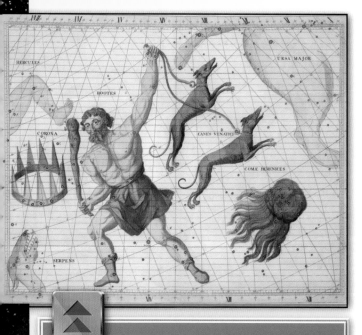

Boötes's dogs are a separate constellation, called Canes Venatici.

People who live in the Northern Hemisphere see certain constellations in the spring. These include Boötes, the Corona Borealis, and Cancer.

Boötes features one of the brightest stars in the sky, Arcturus. The shape of this constellation represents a man holding a spear, club, or staff, with two dogs nearby. The man is called "the herdsman." Different legends state he was the son of different gods.

The semicircular Corona Borealis represents the story of Ariadne, a princess who was rescued from an island by the god Dionysus. He gave her a crown of jewels. When she died, the god threw the crown into the sky.

Cancer the crab is one of the signs of the zodiac. The goddess Hera rewarded a crab by placing it in the sky.

THINK ABOUT IT

How can a constellation, like Boötes, have more than one legend?

Some cultures saw Corona Borealis *(crown, right)* as a broken dish or dancing ladies.

CONSTELLATIONS IN SUMMER

LACERTA, CYGNUS, LYRA, VULPECULA AND ANSER.

Lyra and Cygnus are shown in this group of constellations.

Summer constellations in the Northern Hemisphere include Lyra, Cygnus, and Sagittarius.

The story of Lyra involves Orpheus, who played beautiful music to save his wife. The constellation is seen in the shape of a musical instrument called a lyre, which is like a harp. Lyra contains a bright white star called Vega.

The constellation Cygnus, the swan, is also known as the Northern Cross. According to this story, the Greek god Zeus transformed into a swan to trick a woman into loving him. This constellation contains a very bright star called Deneb.

The constellation Sagittarius represents a centaur, preparing to shoot an arrow from his bow. This constellation points toward the center of the Milky Way galaxy.

Sagittarius is a mythical creature that is half man, half horse.

A **galaxy** is a collection of stars and planets that are pulled together by gravity.

Constellations in Fall

The constellation Perseus, showing Medusa's cut-off head.

Perseus and Pegasus are constellations seen in the fall sky in the Northern Hemisphere.

A son of Zeus, Perseus was famous for killing the monster Medusa. Although Perseus can only be seen for part of the night in the summer months, every year in August a meteor shower seems to come from its northern stars.

Perseus features Algol, the "demon" star. Ancient people feared the star because its light frequently changed in intensity. Astronomers now know Algol is actually two stars, one of which passes in front of the other every few days.

In mythology, Pegasus, the winged horse, went on heroic missions for the gods. The constellation looks like a square with three legs. One of its stars, named 51 Pegasi, has its own planet.

THINK ABOUT IT

As technology improves, what do you think astronomers will discover about the stars in constellations?

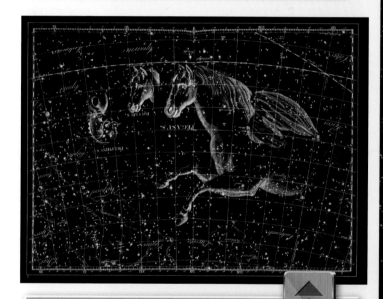

Pegasus is one of the largest constellations. It represents a mythical horse with wings.

CONSTELLATIONS IN WINTER

Orion is one of the most recognizable constellations. It appears in the Northern Hemisphere in the winter.

Orion, hunter for the gods, is the brightest constellation in the winter sky. Its upper stars represent shoulders, and the lower stars are legs. Two arms, one holding a bow, stretch up and out of the shoulders. Many people recognize Orion by the middle three stars, which look like the hunter's belt.

The three stars of Orion's belt are easily seen in the winter sky.

COMPARE AND CONTRAST
Which season do you think is the best for stargazing?
What time of year would give you the best view?

Orion has two dogs behind him—the constellations Canis Major and Canis Minor. Canis Major contains Sirius, the brightest star in the night sky. Canis Minor's brightest star is called Procyon. These two stars, combined with Betelgeuse in Orion, form what's known as the Winter Triangle.

Sirius, the brightest star in the night sky, is visible to the left in this photograph.

GLOSSARY

astronomers Scientists who study space.

celestial Relating to the sky.

centaur A creature that is half man and half horse.

civilizations Well-organized and developed societies that demonstrate a commitment to art, science, and culture.

cultures Particular societies that have their own beliefs, ways of life, art, etc.

cuneiform A system of writing used in parts of the ancient Middle East.

ecliptic The path that the Sun appears to move in as it crosses the sky.

faint Dim or not bright.

latitude An imaginary line around Earth that tells how far north or south of the Equator one is.

legends Stories from the past that are believed by many people but cannot be proved to be true.

navigation The act of finding the right direction.

nomads People who do not have a permanent home.

observations Things that are seen and recorded.

orbit The path taken by one body circling around another body.

ranked Arranged in order.

zodiac A belt of space around Earth. It occupies the path that the Sun appears to take around Earth in the course of a year.

FOR MORE INFORMATION

Books

Forest, Christopher. *The Kids' Guide to the Constellations.* Mankato, MN: Capstone Press, 2012.

Hunter, Nick. *Stars and Constellations.* Chicago, IL: Capstone Heinemann Library, 2014.

Kim, F. S. *Constellations.* New York, NY: Scholastic, 2010.

Peters, Stephanie True. *The Little Dipper.* New York, NY: PowerKids Press, 2003.

Peters, Stephanie True. *Orion.* New York, NY: PowerKids Press, 2003.

Racine, Sheryl, and Kathi Wagner. *The Everything Kids' Astronomy Book.* Avon, MA: Adams Media, 2008.

Zappa, Marcia. *Constellations.* Edina, MN: ABDO Publishing Company, 2011.

Websites

Because of the changing nature of Internet links, Rosen Publishing has developed an online list of websites related to the subject of this book. This site is updated regularly. Please use this link to access the list:

http://www.rosenlinks.com/lfo/const

INDEX